50 YEARS OF THE
DESERT BONEYARD

150324

50 YEARS OF THE DESERT BONEYARD

Davis Monthan A.F.B. Arizona

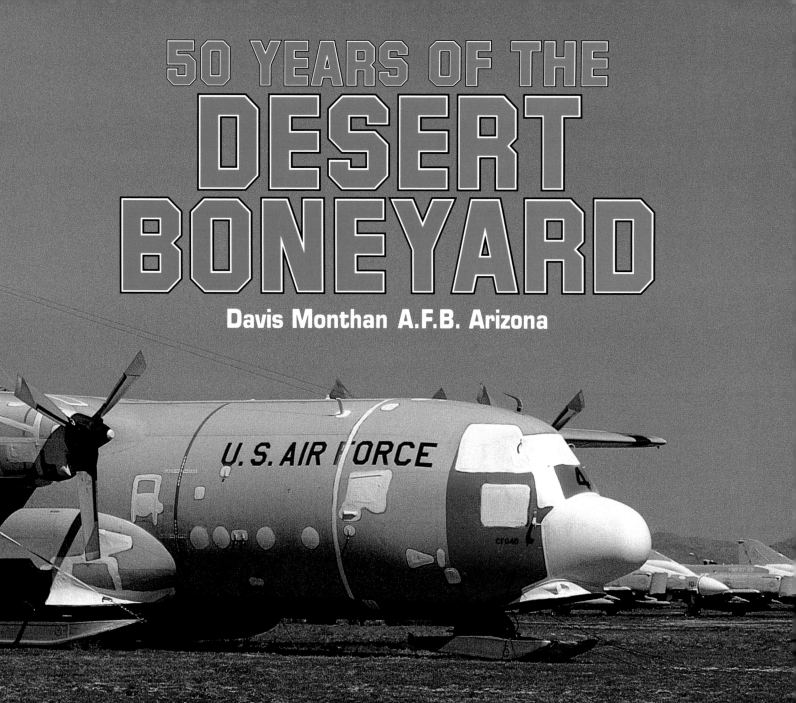

Philip D. Chinnery

Motorbooks International
Publishers & Wholesalers

Acknowledgements

The author would like to thank Andy Anderson, Doug Olson, Patrick Martin, Bob Shane and Ian MacFarlane for their help in the preparation of this book.

CONTENTS

This edition first published in 1995 by Motorbooks International, Publishers & Wholesalers, PO Box 2, 729 Prospect Avenue, Osceola, WI 54020, USA.

© Philip D. Chinnery 1995

Previously published by Airlife Publishing Ltd., Shrewsbury, England, 1995

Library of Congress Cataloging-in-Publication Data is available

ISBN 0-7603-0187–5

Printed in Singapore.

IN THE BEGINNING

The origins of the desert boneyard date back to the end of World War 2, to the days following the abrupt ending of the war with Japan. By the summer of 1945 the American bomber forces in Europe had been stood down following the capitulation of Nazi Germany. In the Pacific, though, the war was expected to drag on for months or possibly years as the Americans island-hopped towards Japan.

The aircraft manufacturers in the United States continued to produce streams of bombers in anticipation of the need to reduce the Japanese cities prior to an all-out invasion of the country by Allied forces. However, the unexpected surrender of Japan, following the exploding of atomic bombs over Nagasaki and Hiroshima, left the United States Army Air Force with vast numbers of aircraft and nothing to do with them.

Towards the end of 1945 the fleets of war-weary aircraft began to return home from the far-flung corners of the globe. By June 1946 almost 34,000 aircraft had arrived at thirty airfields throughout the United States. The majority of them, some 26,700 aircraft, were collected at seven main airfields.

The largest number was stored at Clinton Naval Air Station in Oklahoma: 8,028 Navy aircraft were present, including 1,444 Grumman Wildcats and 1,366 Hellcats. The 5,660 aircraft at Walnut Ridge in Arkansas included 87 B-32 Dominator bombers – nearly the entire production run – that were flown direct to the storage field from the factory at Fort Worth. Kingman Army Air Field in Arizona held almost as many aircraft as Walnut Ridge. Over 5,500 aircraft arrived, of which roughly one third were B-17s, one third B-24s and the rest made up of various types including the A-20, B-25, B-26, P-38 and P-63. The three other main storage centres were at Altus in Oklahoma (2,543 aircraft), Albuquerque in New Mexico (1,706) and Vernon in Texas (1,322).

With the development of the jet engine, many of the aircraft were fast becoming obsolete and there were just too many aircraft of all types to fulfil the peace-time needs of the United States' armed forces. Consequently the decision was made to scrap or sell to the public the bulk of aircraft in storage. The War Assets Administration and the Reconstruction Finance Corporation were instructed to arrange the disposal of over $9,900,000,000 worth of aircraft. Transport and trainer types could be sold to the general public, but the majority of the combat types, the fighters and bombers, were of no further use. Soon $8,000,000

worth of aircraft was being scrapped and melted down into metal ingots every day.

One notable exception to the rule was Boeing's B-29 Superfortress bomber, the type that had carried the atomic bombs to Japan. The most modern bomber in the Air Force inventory was to be retained and a war-reserve created. The Iron Curtain was now descending across Europe and the Cold War had begun. Some surplus aircraft were to be kept in reserve, just in case. A handful of bases in the south-western United States were chosen as storage depots, but their existences were all short-lived, except for Davis-Monthan Air Force Base in Arizona, which is still in use today.

The original 640 acres of land on which Davis-Monthan Air Force Base now stands was purchased from the state land department in 1925 for $19.50. The citizens of Tucson named the base in honour of Lieutenants Samuel H. Davis and Oscar Monthan, both Air Corps officers from Tucson. Davis was killed in Florida in 1921 and Monthan died in Honolulu in 1923, both in military accidents. After Pearl Harbor the base was expanded and soon rated as one of the best heavy bombardment training stations in the land. Its location in the Arizona desert made it ideal for year-round training and this was taken into account when the search began for a B-29 and C-47 storage base.

The main reason for its choice was the climate. Annual rainfall was low – around eleven inches per year – and humidity was low too, between ten and twenty per cent. In addition, the soil, known as 'caliche' has a low acidic content and is baked so hard by the sun that aircraft can be parked on it, without needing tarmac or concrete stands.

The last B-29 training unit was deactivated at Davis-Monthan in October 1945 and the base transferred to the jurisdiction of the San Antonio Air Technical Service Command (SAATSC). The 4105th Army Air Force Base Unit (Air Base) was activated to oversee the new storage centre, and by 10 January 1946 the first C-47s and B-29s had arrived.

By the end of 1946, 679 B-29s and 241 C-47s were in storage. There were also 30 other aircraft earmarked, with remarkable foresight, for museum preservation. They included the two B-29s *Enola Gay* and *Bockscar* that had dropped the atomic bombs on Japan; the sole XB-19, which until the advent of the B-36 was the largest aircraft built for the Air Force; the Beechcraft A-38 Destroyer experimental attack plane with a 75mm cannon in a long, sharp pointed nose and a captured German Ju88.

Beginning in 1947, an interesting

experiment in the preservation of B-29s in the desert environment was carried out. Called 'cocooning', the process was performed by the Fort Pitt Packaging Company under 8th Air Force guidelines. Each B-29 in storage was worth over half a million dollars and to protect them it was decided to cocoon them in airtight cases. The cocoons consisted of two layers of plastic and a sealer known as Insulmastic No. 4500, a Gilsonite product. It was seven times stronger than rawhide and was designed to keep out dirt and moisture for at least ten years. The Fort Pitt Packaging Company was awarded the contract to cocoon 486 of the 679 B-29s then in storage and work began in July 1947. Each aircraft was washed and many bags of moisture-absorbing dessicant were placed inside them. The propellers and engine cowlings were covered with masking tape and a first coat of yellow plastic was applied by spray guns to the outside of the aircraft. This was followed by a second, red coat; the colour was changed to ensure complete coverage of all areas of the aircraft. The black Insulmastic sealer followed and then a final coat of aluminium paint was applied to reflect most of the heat from the sun.

In May 1948 the Cocooning Project was terminated after 447 B-29s had been treated. Problems soon arose with blisters appearing in the cocoons as air trapped under the cocooning expanded during the heat of the day and broke the seal of the plastic. In addition, when some aircraft were prepared for return to service, up to 600 man hours were required to strip the cocoons from each aircraft. Clearly, for future preservation projects, a more suitable method had to be found.

On 28 August 1948 the designation of the 4105th was changed to the 3040th Aircraft Storage Depot, with reclamation (spare parts removal) and salvage added to the mission. Forty-seven B-29s and 14 of the museum aircraft were earmarked for reclamation, and with further withdrawals due to East–West tension over the Berlin blockade the inventory at the end of the year had dropped to 535 B-29s and 187 C-47s. If the figure of 535 B-29s in storage is compared to the 470 then operational with Strategic Air Command, the size of the B-29 war reserve at Davis-Monthan can be imagined.

The Berlin blockade ended in September 1949 without SAC needing to go to war. A shortage of C-47 spare parts in the Air Force and the supply of C-47s to various South American governments reduced the number of C-47s in storage by half. The year 1950 also saw two-thirds of the B-29s return to service. Eighty-seven were loaned to the Royal Air Force as a stop-gap replacement between the demise of the ageing Lincolns and the arrival of the modern Canberra and V-bomber aircraft. They were designated Washington B Mk 1s and served with nine RAF squadrons until returning to the desert in 1954.

On 25 June 1950, North Korean military forces invaded South Korea and within days the lightly armed South Korean Army was in full retreat. One week later, SAC's 22nd and 92nd Bomb Groups were ordered to fly to bases in Okinawa and Japan to prepare for conventional bombing missions in Korea, north of the 38th Parallel which divided the two countries. America was at war again and replacement aircraft would be required to replace those lost in combat. Two weeks after the start of hostilities, Headquarters, Air Materiel Command directed the withdrawal from storage of 50 B-29s for overhaul and reconditioning by the Grand Central Aircraft Company at Tucson Airport.

The Korean war led to a vast expansion of SAC's bomber fleet. By the end of the year the workforce at the 3040th was working flat-out to return stored B-29s to service and to reclaim those too old to return to active service. Spare parts worth over $300,000, half the initial cost of each aircraft, were being removed from each B-29; these included bombsights, engines, fuel and oil tanks, propellers and instruments. When the aircraft were reduced to stripped-out carcasses they were sold for scrap at $2,300 each.

After disassembly the centre of gravity of a B-29 changed drastically, so fifteen-feet-long, one-foot-square timbers were tied to the nose wheel-well of the aircraft and as many as 25 personnel were loaded into the nose section compartments. The aircraft would then be towed one and a half miles out to the storage area for 'demilitarisation' prior to sale as scrap. Demilitarisation meant cutting the tail section off the B-29. Heavy cables would be looped over the tail assembly by a crane and attached to a heavy cleat track. The track would take-off fast and the cable would contract, slicing the 6,000-pound tail assembly off on to a trailer underneath.

By the end of December 1951 only 172 cocooned and 65 non-cocooned B-29s were left in storage. The Strategic Air Command had reached its peak of 540 B-29 bombers, plus 84 reconnaissance versions and 256 converted to aerial refuelling tankers. However, the first Boeing B-47 Stratojet bomber had now entered service, joining the other more modern SAC bombers, the B-36s and B-50s. For the ageing B-29, the writing was on the wall.

Having spent the last couple of years returning hundreds of B-29s to service, the 3040th was about to start receiving them

all back again. On 1 April 1953 HQ, Air Materiel Command instructed the storage centre to commence a number of major projects, including the processing of 440 B-29s into storage. In July, as the war in Korea drew to an uneasy close, the first 24 Superfortresses arrived.

With the uneasy ending of the Korean war and the modernisation of SAC's bomber fleet, the B-29 was no longer required. SAC was now equipping with the B-36 Peacemaker and B-47 Stratojet, and even the KB-29 aerial refuelling tanker squadrons were now outnumbered twenty to eight by the new KC-97 Stratotanker squadrons. As the war-weary bombers began to return to Davis-Monthan, other types also started to arrive. By the end of 1953, 120 North American T-6 Texan trainers, 29 Grumman SA-16 Albatross amphibians and 21 Boeing QB-17s had arrived. The QB-17s were Flying Fortresses converted as radio-controlled drones and used as unmanned airborne targets.

With ever-increasing numbers of aircraft arriving for storage, more land was required. Consequently a further 480 acres of land was purchased, increasing the size of the storage centre to 1,290 acres.

1954 was to be the busiest year for the storage centre since its establishment nine years previously. As the weeks passed, project followed project; to prepare aircraft for storage, to strip them for spare parts or to prepare them for fly-away. However, no sooner had a project commenced than it was changed again. It became obvious that the project directors at HQ AMC and HQ USAF needed to get their act together. One such example was project MDA4T of 23 April 1954 which required 57 of the T-6 trainers to be taken out of storage and prepared for departure. The departure schedule was changed four times and in the end only 47 aircraft were required.

Over 30 various projects were commenced during the year. In February a Navy project was begun involving the dispatch of ten B-29s to the New Mexico Institute of Mining and Technology at Scocorro in New Mexico, for vulnerability tests. 16,830 man-hours were needed to prepare the aircraft and all were dismantled and shipped overland. Parts of these B-29s, including the remains of a former RAF Washington B1, are still to be found at Scocorro today.

In March the first two Boeing B-50 bombers arrived for storage and were due to be followed by 259 others, although the total was soon reduced to 194. By July, work had begun on removing the APS/23 radar sets and APA/44 computers from 77 B-50Ds, and in December the 3040th was instructed to remove 75 more for a one-time flight to Hayes Industries of

Birmingham, Alabama following a decision to convert a number of the B-50s to aerial refuelling tankers.

The demise of the B-29 fleet began early in the year when work started on reclaiming 183 of those in storage. Their R-3350-23A engines were not needed and remained on the aircraft to be sold as scrap. By the time the last RAF B-29, 44-62259, arrived in September, a further 240 B-29s had been earmarked for salvage.

Both the Army and the Navy became involved in the fate of some of the B-29s towards the end of 1954. In August, a 'blast test' project was commenced by Army explosive experts from the Aberdeen Proving Grounds in Maryland. Ninety B-29s were used for the tests, which involved the latest developments in explosives. After the explosions, the base fire truck would extinguish any fires and studies would be made to assess the vulnerability and effectual damage to structural areas of the aircraft. In November, a Navy representative from Inyokern, California arrived to arrange the removal of a number of B-29s by one-time flight to the Navy Proving Grounds at China Lake. Fortunately, some of the China Lake B-29s and a handful that were taken back to the Aberdeen Proving Grounds survived and have subsequently found their way into various museums.

By June 1954 the inventory of aircraft in storage totalled 1,205 aircraft, as follows: 62 SA-16s, 27 B-17s, one B-24, one Ju 88, 465 B-29s, 120 B-50s, ten L-20s, ten L-23s and 509 T-6s. Soon to arrive were four YC-97 Stratofreighters, although they would be held in temporary storage for departure in the near future. SAC's last B-29 bomber, 'A' model 42-94032, from the 307th Bomb Wing, arrived at Davis-Monthan on 4 November.

Very little information exists concerning the activities of the 3040th during 1955 and the first half of 1956. However, it is known that the first Douglas B-26 bomber, Curtiss C-46 Commando transport and North American F-86 Sabre arrived during that time. Also, 120 of the B-29s were scrapped during the eighteen-month period.

On 1 June 1956 the 3040th Aircraft Storage Squadron (renamed in 1949 from 'Depot') at Davis-Monthan Air Force Base was renamed the Arizona Aircraft Storage Branch (AASB). The change of name meant little to the workers at the centre. Their main concern now was to accelerate the disposal of the 350 B-29s still in storage. The space that they occupied would soon be required because the first of the giant Convair B-36 Peacemaker bombers was about to arrive.

A very rare aerial photograph of the early days of the Desert Boneyard, showing C-47s parked in pairs at the top, with rows of B-29s to the right and thirty museum-type aircraft in the foreground. Sadly many of the latter were scrapped. *(Harry Gann)*

(OPPOSITE)
In the beginning ...Colonel R. Frank Schirmer, the first commander of Air Materiel Command's 4105th Army Air Force Base Unit, Aircraft Storage, in 1945. *(Via Frank Schirmer)*

Weary Rebel, Boeing B-29A Superfortress *42-24467* in storage in 1945. *(Frank Schirmer)*

Early Days. Taken by Colonel Frank Schirmer, base commander in 1946, this photograph shows the cocooning method used to preserve B-29s after World War 2. Removing the material was a laborious job. *(Frank Schirmer)*

Douglas XB-19 *8471*, the largest aircraft of its time, shares the storage area with dozens of B-29s in 1946. It was eventually scrapped. *(Frank Schirmer)*

Pacusan Dreamboat, a Boeing B-29 Superfortress, held the record for the longest flight in 1945 and was stored at the 4105th AAFBU after the war.
(Pima Air Museum)

Some of the Air Force stock of Boeing B-29 Superfortress bombers were sent to the Naval Weapons Centre at China Lake, California in 1955 for use as ground targets. The author photographed the last five survivors there in 1986.

MASDC AND THE VIETNAM YEARS

The first of the giant B-36 Peacemaker bombers began to arrive at the Arizona Aircraft Storage Branch in the summer of 1956. Ten GRB-36Ds were amongst the first to arrive, followed by the RB-36Ds and Es of the 99th Strategic Reconnaissance Wing and B-36Ds of the 92nd Bomb Wing. Both Wings were based at Fairchild AFB, Washington and ceased B-36 operations between September and November 1956.

A reclamation project began immediately to strip certain spare parts from the new arrivals and return them to the Air Force inventory for use on B-36s still in service. Thirty-nine B-36s were released to the Mar-Pak Corporation, under contract to the Air Force, for reclamation and removal of certain items. A year later, with stripped-out carcasses littering the desert, a smelter was constructed to melt down the unwanted wrecks.

Around this time, Air Materiel Command instructed the AASB to perform a processing and reclamation test on ten B-36s to determine exactly how many hours were required to reclaim each aircraft. B-36F *49-2681* was the first of the ten to arrive, braking to a halt at the end of the Davis-Monthan runway at 1045 hours on 3 June 1957. The aircraft was defuelled to 1,000 gallons and then towed to the industrial area where all loose items were removed, together with the guns and specialised equipment. The remaining fuel and all the oils were then drained and the aircraft was parked and tied down. The civilian engineers set to work with their 'save lists', removing the parts required, such as the propellers and tyres. The parts were then cleaned, inspected and sent out to various storage depots. Sixteen days were required to transform *49-2681* from a front-line strategic bomber into a derelict carcass. The test proved that, although it took 942 man hours per aircraft and a total cost of $28,930 in labour and materials, the ten aircraft yielded 7,106 spare parts, with a stock value of $7,750,000. With such savings to be made, the AASB was truly in business.

Within a month, the AASB was advised that, due to the forthcoming phase-out of the remaining Peacemakers, requirements for parts and components to be saved should rapidly diminish and incoming aircraft were placed in temporary storage. The next couple of years saw more work arrive than the storage centre could handle as Air Force Project Streamline IIIR got underway. This involved the withdrawal from service of 7,000 aircraft by the end of 1961.

Disposal of surplus aircraft took on a new priority and soon three civilian-operated smelters were in action, one owned by Air Associates to dispose of B-29 and B-50 carcasses and the two others, owned by Mar-Pak and Page Airways, were concentrating on 230 acres of B-36 carcasses. Alongside the contractors' smelters their guillotines were working overtime. These consisted of 8,500 pounds of armour plate dropped from seventy-five feet from the boom of a crane in order to sever parts of the wings and fuselage and cut them into easily handled pieces to feed into the smelters.

Foreign military sales also took place, with T-28s going to the Mexican Air Force, B-26s to Brazil and T-6s to France. Distribution of excess aircraft to other government agencies and other branches of the military, or donations to eligible organisations or groups, was now an alternative to automatic disposal in the furnaces of the smelters.

The peak of the Streamline IIIR aircraft phase-out took place during 1959 and 1960. In the twelve months to June 1959, 652 more aircraft arrived, including the 432nd and last B-36 Peacemaker and 43 B-47 Stratojet bombers. Amongst the aircraft movements was the arrival of B-29 *45-21800*, which had been modified to carry Chuck Yeager's experimental Bell X-1 aloft, and the departure of B-36J *52-2220*, which made the last Peacemaker flight on 29 April 1959 when it flew out of Davis-Monthan to the site of the new Air Force Museum at Wright-Patterson Air Force Base, Ohio.

On 1 August 1959 the Arizona Aircraft Storage Branch was redesignated the 2704th Air Force Aircraft Storage and Disposition Group (AFASDG) and began to report direct to HQ, Air Materiel Command. In the same month, 110 C-46 cargo aircraft and 94 B-26 bombers went on sale.

As the Air Force squadrons continued to disband, 500 more North American F-86 Sabres arrived, together with the first examples of the Century Series of fighters: the F-100 Super Sabre, F-101 Voodoo, F-104 Starfighter and F-105 Thunderchief. The first B-57 Canberra and B-66 Destroyer bombers arrived and the number of B-47 Stratojet bombers being retired also increased as Boeing's new B-52 Stratofortress came into service.

Almost 2,000 more arrivals brought the June 1960 inventory up to over 4,000 aircraft, despite 1,000 more aircraft being scrapped in the meantime. These included 375 F-84s which were, at one time, piled three or four high awaiting disposal. The last WB-29 Weather Service aircraft were retired in 1960 and were the last B-29s to go to Davis-Monthan for disposal. The Boeing B-29 Superfortress, which had first flown in 1942, had at last reached the end of the line. Today, out of 3,960 B-29s produced, less than 36 still survive, including *44-86292 Enola Gay*, immortalised as the aircraft that dropped the first atomic bomb on Hiroshima on 6 August 1945. The bomb, dubbed 'Little Boy', contained the power of 20,000 tons of TNT and destroyed 4.7 square miles of the city, killing or injuring 140,000 people. Another B-29 to escape the smelter is *Bockscar* which dropped a second atomic bomb, 'Fat Man', on Nagasaki on 9 August 1945. The casualties and damage, although fewer and less than at Hiroshima, coupled with the Soviet Union's declaration of war on Japan the previous day and the months of B-29 attacks on Japanese cities, finally convinced the Japanese to surrender unconditionally.

The last B-36 sale took place in May 1960 and included all remaining Peacemakers. The magnitude of the disposal programme taking place, can be imagined when one realises that this last B-36 carcass sale amounted to 2,800 tons of scrap metal and the lot was sold for over half a million dollars. The last carcass had been smelted by 2 October 1961 and the once mighty Peacemaker fleet ceased to exist. When the dust had settled and the furnaces had cooled, only five B-36s remained, preserved at various air bases.

Headquarters, Air Materiel Command was now aware of the potential value of its Davis-Monthan storage centre; over one twelve-month period, $64 million worth of spare parts had been returned to Air Force stocks. As a result, they authorised the construction of a new industrial complex and an increase in staff to 737 civilians and fourteen military personnel. Half a million dollars was spent on a new reclamation building with a 918-feet-long roof, which not only protected the workers from the desert sun but provided 180,000 square feet of shelter to house the reclamation processing, packaging, crating and shipping functions.

The reclamation shelter changed the entire pattern of routine reclamation. Aircraft would henceforth be towed to the shelter and workers would carry out their tasks under its shade instead of beneath the withering direct sun of Arizona's desert. No longer would all reclaimed parts jolt around in the back of a truck for up to a mile, between the aircraft from which they had been taken and the location where cleaning, sorting and other steps prior to shipment were to take place.

In April 1961, Air Materiel Command was split into two parts: the Air Force Systems Command and the Air Force Logistics Command. The 2704th now reported directly to HQ AFLC. By this time, 300 more B-47 Stratojets had arrived and six more Bomb Wings were scheduled for deactivation.

In the summer of 1961, strained relations between the United States and the Soviet Union over Berlin led to the decision to postpone the planned deactivation of six Bomb Wings of B-47s and six Air Refuelling Squadrons of KC-97 tankers. The discovery by a SAC U-2 spyplane of Soviet ballistic missiles being installed in Cuba in October resulted in President Kennedy placing Strategic Air Command on full alert, and the 2704th halted all B-47 reclamation and prepared to return a large number to service if required. Fortunately, SAC did not need to go to war, and with the delivery of its last B-52 and B-58 Hustler bombers the retirement of the remaining B-47s could begin in earnest. The 2704th was ready for the influx of Stratojets; it had now expanded to 1,744 acres and with a mere 2,700 aircraft in storage in June 1963 it had room to spare.

In 1964 yet another money-saving proposal by the Department of Defense led to the closure of the Navy aircraft storage centre at Litchfield Park, 150 miles north of Davis-Monthan. Its function was to be combined with that of the 2704th as a single manager operation, and to reflect its new multi-service role the centre was redesignated on 1 February 1965 the Military Aircraft Storage and Disposition Center (MASDC).

The mission of the renamed centre was defined as 'the processing and maintaining of aircraft in storage; preparation of aircraft for one-time flight or transfer; reclamation of aircraft/aircraft engines and components for inventory replenishment and/or special projects; processing of aircraft/aircraft engines and residue for disposal; administration of sales and/or service contracts with foreign governments, other government agencies and commercial contractors'.

To ensure that their interests would be taken care of, the Navy opened a Field Service Office at MASDC and the transfer of 800 aircraft from Litchfield Park began. Five hundred of the aircraft were moved by truck, because of the cost involved to strip away each aircraft's preservative and prepare it for a 150-mile flight to MASDC. It cost $350 per aircraft and saved more than a million dollars.

A further 1,000 acres was added to MASDC, for a total of 2,729 acres, and this more than accommodated the 2,000 Air Force and 800 Navy aircraft and the first early-model B-52 bombers which began to arrive in May 1965.

The United States was now involved in a 'shooting war' in south-east Asia and the search was on for a suitable counter-insurgency aircraft that could fly low and slow and carry a heavy bomb load. The spotlight fell on MASDC and soon nearly 400 surplus Navy A-1 Skyraiders, Air Force B-26 Bombers and T-28 Trojan trainers were being withdrawn from storage and sent to overhaul depots where they would be modified for their new ground-attack role. In addition, the planned expansion of the South Vietnamese Air Force led to the transfer of C-47s, A-1s and T-28s from MASDC stocks.

A use was found for the lines of vintage C-47 'Gooney Bird' transports sitting in the desert. The Air Force withdrew 33 from storage, fitted them with three 7.62mm mini-guns in the port windows and cargo door and sent them to Vietnam. With each gun capable of firing 6,000 rounds per minute, the AC-47 gunships were used by Air Commando Squadrons to protect Special Forces camps and isolated outposts. Known by their callsign 'Spooky', they were also dubbed 'Puff, the Magic Dragon' by those who had witnessed the streams of tracer rounds pouring through the darkness towards the ground, as the aircraft flew a left-hand pylon turn around the target.

As the war escalated and the Air Force began to carry the war into North Vietnam, seven RB-66B Destroyers were dispatched from MASDC to join those already in Thailand and South Vietnam. The B-52 bombers based on Guam were now flying daily 'Arc Light' missions against the Viet Cong and the wear and tear on their engines led to a request to MASDC for two dozen J57-29 power packs, to be removed from B-52Bs in storage. In the twelve months to June 1966, MASDC shipped 51,000 spare parts and engines in support of the war.

Between 1945 and 1966, 14,000 aircraft had arrived at Davis-Monthan AFB and only 2,800 had flown out again. Very few aircraft of World War 2 vintage were now left at MASDC. One of the last, a DB-17P Drone Director aircraft, departed on a five-year lease to the International Flight and Space Museum in Ontario, California. Ironically, Ontario received 2,000 surplus aircraft at the war's end and the majority, including of course the B-17s, were scrapped.

On 28 June 1966 MASDC received a new far-sighted and imaginative commander, Colonel I.R. Perkin. He immediately set to work improving the image of the storage centre. With the aim of publicising the work of MASDC and its value to the taxpayer, a brochure and twenty-minute film were produced, appropriately titled *Desert Bonanza*. The new commander also arranged a display of a number of museum-type stored aircraft along the perimeter fence where they could be seen by the general public. This was the forerunner of today's 'Celebrity Row'. He was also a driving force behind the idea of

an air museum for Tucson. Eventually a site was chosen for the Pima Air Museum and the 35 aircraft on display on the base were moved there. The collection has now grown to over 200 aircraft and the museum receives around 100,000 visitors each year. A unique arrangement with the storage centre allows the museum to display aircraft on loan from 'across the road' and is guaranteed a good supply of exhibits for the foreseeable future.

Inter-service transfers were now commonplace and one such agreement involved the transfer of 28 Navy EC-121 airborne early warning aircraft to the Air Force for use in south-east Asia. The Air Force was also in dire need of replacement engines for its bombers, so 266 B-52 and B-66 engines were shipped out. By now the sixty early-model B-52s in storage had been virtually picked clean and within a year all would have been scrapped.

The Air Force was also retiring large numbers of reciprocating-engined cargo and transport aircraft such as the C-117, C-118 and T-29. The cost and scarcity of high octane fuel contributed to their replacement by jet-engined aircraft. A large number of the T-29s would eventually find their way on to the civilian airline market. Another type affected was the C-124 Globemaster fleet, which was also suffering from wing defects. All but a handful of these huge transports had their engines removed and were later broken up.

The Navy had now retired its A-1E Skyraiders and 53 were transferred to the Air Force for use by the Special Operations Squadrons (formerly Air Commando Squadrons) over Laos and for providing Search and Rescue escort throughout the theatre of war. A tough aircraft, the Skyraider was ideal for the ground support role and four Air Force squadrons flew the type in south-east Asia.

By 1968 some of the older types of aircraft began to return to MASDC from the South Vietnamese Air Force. These were C-47D transports and H-34 helicopters and one or two were still to be found at Davis-Monthan in the mid-1980s. Norway had already returned three dozen F-86 Sabres supplied under the Military Assistance Programme and these were now joined by seven C-119G transports, all of which would be broken up and scrapped. The Army had begun to use MASDC shortly after the Navy moved in from Litchfield Park; now the Coast Guard appeared on the scene, retiring the first two of their HU-16 Albatross amphibians.

The 1969 inventory stood at 3,576 aircraft and helicopters. Approximately 67 per cent were in storage, 15 per cent were awaiting reclamation, ten per cent were hulks awaiting sale for scrap and seven per cent were of the Reclamation Insurance

Type (RIT) status. The latter category applied to certain aircraft set aside as a source of spare parts, to keep active aircraft flying. Reclamation of the 1,000 B-47 Stratojets retired by SAC had begun in December 1967 and by June 1969 over 300 had been scrapped. Eventually the whole fleet would be sold for scrap to Allied Aircraft Sales of Tucson.

Strategic Air Command began to retire their two B-58 Hustler Bomb Wings in November 1969 and within three months all 84 were in storage. A couple were earmarked for museums, but the rest were sold to Southwestern Alloys in 1977 and broken up for scrap.

Metal fatigue was also plaguing the C-133 Cargomaster fleet, which had been in service since 1957 and was often used to transport Atlas, Thor and Jupiter missiles. The fifty-strong fleet was purchased in 1973 by Allied Aircraft Sales and Kolar Incorporated, who sold a handful as potentially flyable and fed the rest into their smelters. The pollution caused by the smelters led the Pima County Air Pollution Control department to complain about their use, and as a result contractors were now required to remove all aircraft carcasses to off-base smelters, where they would come under the jurisdiction of pollution control officials.

In accordance with President Richard Nixon's policy of 'Vietnamisation', the United States had begun to withdraw from south-east Asia and was attempting to bolster the Air Forces of the countries still under threat from the North Vietnamese. Four dozen C-123 Providers were shipped to South Vietnam, including 16 from MASDC, and ten UH-34G helicopters left for Laos to be used by Air America, the clandestine airline run by the Central Intelligence Agency to support the anti-communist forces in the country.

The American expertise in converting aircraft to gunships was used to produce 13 AU-23A gunship versions of the Pilatus Turbo-Porter, which were sent to Thailand from MASDC for counter-insurgency operations. Fourteen AU-24A Helio Courier gunships were sent to Cambodia where they were used with great success against the Khmer Rouge.

With the winding-down of the war MASDC received notification of Operations Plan 'Pacer Harvest', which provided guidance for the expected input of aircraft after the American withdrawal. Amongst the first aircraft to arrive were P-2 and C-123 gunships. The three AP-2H Neptunes were from Navy Heavy Attack Squadron VAH-21, based at Cam Rahn Bay, from where they had flown over 200 missions using their guns and bombs on enemy road and river traffic in the Mekong Delta. Two 'Black Spot' NC-123K Providers also arrived for removal of classified equipment, used in testing new systems for future designs of gunships. They were then passed on to the Thai Air Force who were in need of transport aircraft.

By June 1971 the total number of aircraft in storage had risen to 4,605, including 400 TH-55A training helicopters from the recently closed Army helicopter training establishment at Fort Wolters in Texas. The B-47 fleet had been reduced to 56 aircraft and reclamation had begun on 200 F-102 Delta Daggers.

The end of 1971 saw the centre covered in five inches of snow, an unusual and unexpected occurrence. It remained for a whole day before the desert sun got the better of it. A request for a hard surface work ramp in the industrial area for the preparation of aircraft for flight was turned down due to the estimated cost of three million dollars. However, MASDC was made the distribution centre for AM-2 matting that had been used in Vietnam for temporary airfields. Four hundred truck loads provided the centre with a 183,000-square-yard apron, the largest in the world at that time.

In the twelve months to June 1973 2,130 aircraft had arrived for storage, bringing the total to an all-time high of 6,080 aircraft and missiles. Approximately 2,500 were Air Force, 1,900 Navy, 1,500 Army and six Coast Guard. The problem now was what to do with them all.

Douglas C-124C Globemaster *52-1069* was modified as a turbo-prop engine test-bed. It cost $1,646,406 and spare parts worth $1,423,864 were removed before it was scrapped. This photograph was taken in May 1959. *(Pima Air Museum)*

A field of Convair B-36 Peacemakers await their fate. RB-36H *50-1110*, nearest, is wearing the badge of the 5th Bombardment Wing *(Heavy)* with 'Kia-O-Ka-Lewa' Guardian of the Upper Regions underneath.

(Doug Olson)

(LEFT)
One of many Navy Skyraiders still preserved in storage in 1969, EA-1F *135034 Jackpot* served with Navy Airborne Early Warning Squadron VAW-13 prior to retirement.
(Author's Collection)

(BELOW)
A typical scene at MASDC in the early 1960s, including Boeing KC-97F *51-0222* and Boeing RB-50G Superfortress *47-0147* undergoing spare parts reclamation. *(Author's Collection)*

Douglas C-124C Globemaster *II 52-1022* of the 164th Military Airlift Group, Tennessee ANG was amongst 100 of the type retired in 1972.

(Henry F. Carter)

Rows of Navy Skyraiders and Army
Sikorsky CH-19 Chickasaw helicopters
awaiting destruction in the mid-1950s.
(Author's Collection)

(LEFT)
Colonel I.R. Perkins, commander at MASDC, inspects the bomb mission artwork on a B-52 in March 1967. The identity of *BC046* has not been recorded. *(Author's Collection)*

(BELOW)
Still around in 1969, a line of North American F-86 Sabres with L model *53-0816* from the Iowa Air National Guard nearest the camera.
(Author's Collection)

(RIGHT)
Strategic Air Command Boeing B-47E Stratojet *53-2028* was photographed still fully preserved in 1967, not long before the fleet was finally scrapped.
(Author's Collection)

(BELOW)
This colourfulMartin EB-57E Canberra *55-4253* arrived for storage in July 1979. Note the Aerospace Defense command badge on the tail and the 17th Defense Systems Evaluation Squadron badge on the rear fuselage.
(Philip Chinnery)

(ABOVE)
Colourful Navy Sikorsky SH-34J Sea Horse *148946*/3H007 arrived in April 1969 after service with HT-8. It has since been sold for scrap.
(Philip Chinnery)

(LEFT)
Produced as a cheap gunship conversion for countries such as Cambodia, Fairchild AU-24A Helio Stallion *72-1322* was seen at MASDC in July 1972. *(Patrick Martin/Larsen)*

(RIGHT)
A Boeing B-52 Stratofortress being dismantled in the early 1960s while a C-97 waits for its turn. *(Philip Chinnery)*

(BELOW)
A row of derelict Navy Douglas C-54 Skymasters in December 1969. *(Pima Air Museum)*

Lockheed F-104A Starfighter *56-0826* arrived for storage in January 1968 and was purchased for scrap by Allied Aircraft of Tucson in April 1980.

(Author's Collection)

Boeing WB-50D Superfortress *49-0351* arrived at MASDC in March 1965 and was given to the Pima Air Museum seven years later. It was transferred to the Castle Air Force Base Museum in 1980. *(Author's Collection)*

(LEFT)
This General Dynamics F-111A *65-5709* arrived at MASDC in January 1972 and was photographed on its way overland to Kirtland AFB, New Mexico on 27 September 1973.
(Pima Air Museum)

Douglas F-10B Skynight *124610* was modified by the installation of an F-4B Phantom nose, prior to retirement in August 1968. Transferred to the Army and used as a spare parts machine, the aircraft has recently left AMARC.
(Author's Collection)

A very picturesque scene of Boeing B-52 Stratofortresses against the backdrop of the Santa Catalina Mountains in January 1972. B-52C *53-0402* arrived in late 1971 from the 22nd Bomb Wing. *(Author's Collection)*

A DECADE OF DISPOSAL

Although South Vietnam was not overrun by the North Vietnamese communists until 1975, the United States' involvement came to an end in January 1973. Many aircraft were left behind for the South Vietnamese Air Force, but the majority returned to the United States, many destined for retirement. With 6,080 aircraft in storage at MASDC in 1973, the problem facing the Department of Defense planners was, what to do with them all?

One suggestion involved the replacement of the Air Force's sub-scale Firebee One and Two aerial targets with life-size surplus aircraft. The F-102 Delta Dagger possessed a marked silhouette likeness to the enemy Su-19, MiG-19 and MiG-25, and they were available off-the-shelf from MASDC. The Air Force awarded the Sperry Corporation a contract in 1973 to convert 215 F-102s into remote-controlled target drones. The rebuild programme was called 'Pave Deuce' and the F-102s were de-preserved and ferried to the Sperry facility at Crestview, Florida and, from 1978 onwards, to their Litchfield Park factory near Phoenix. They were then stripped out and modified to fly by remote control, ending their days by being shot down over missile ranges in the New Mexico desert, and over the Gulf of Mexico.

The vast increase in the Army helicopter inventory, as a result of the Vietnam War, meant that they could now do away with some of the older types in storage at MASDC. Consequently 1974 saw the first sale of some of the 500 H-13 Sioux and 400 H-23 Raven training and observation helicopters. A large number were sold to civilian owners and many more were supplied to various state agencies such as Forestry Departments, Civil Defense units, Police Departments and, for instruction purposes, to technical colleges and schools.

The Navy had 300 trainer versions of the F-9 Cougar carrier-based fighter in storage. The type had first flown in 1951 and was now obsolete. Southwestern Alloys purchased the first 100 offered for sale as scrap in 1974 and Sun Valley Aviation bought the remainder two years later. The Navy also had over 100 T-1 Sea Star deck-landing trainers that were now obsolete. They went on sale in the summer of 1974 and were all purchased for scrap by Allied Aircraft Sales.

To prevent combat-type aircraft falling into the wrong hands, they have to be demilitarised prior to removal from the centre. This process simply requires the purchaser to cut the wings and tail assembly off, thus rendering future reassembly and flight impossible.

Generally speaking, transport aircraft and helicopters can be sold intact and can therefore command a higher price. They have usually been subject to spare parts reclamation though and need careful restoration before certification by the FAA. One such type was the C-54 Skymaster, the military version of the four-engined DC-4 commercial transport aircraft. The first of eighty went on sale in 1974, with many being purchased for conversion to fire-fighting water bombers.

Aircraft still arrived for storage, although in fewer numbers than before. One interesting type to arrive was the WB-57F Canberra, eight of which had been retired following the disbandment of the 58th Weather Reconnaissance Squadron on 1 July 1974. They had been greatly modified with new wings of 122-feet span, twice that of normal, and two huge TF-33 turbofan engines. They were used for very high altitude reconnaissance and air sampling duties and a handful are still preserved in storage today.

The last two C-124 Globemasters also arrived during the year from the Georgia Air National Guard. One of the pair left in August 1975 for the USAF Museum and the rest of the fleet, minus their engines and undercarriages, was sold in 1976 for scrap. The second of the pair also escaped the axe and was sold to a civilian buyer, who flew it to Las Vegas, Nevada, and had it painted blue and white. It has remained there ever since. Another transport type which began its retirement in 1974 was the Convair T-29, and 86 arrived during the year. They continued to arrive until the end of 1975, when there were 300 of them in storage. The following year the sales of the type began and many found their way on to the civil market. The Air National Guard also retired its last fifty F-100C Super Sabres during 1974. At the end of 1975 the first of 350 D and F models would begin to arrive, earmarked to follow in the footsteps of the last F-102s.

The year 1975 saw the final collapse of South Vietnam, but not before over 120 South Vietnamese Air Force aircraft had flown out to Thailand. These included 25 A-37B Dragonfly ground attack aircraft, which were sent to MASDC in June and July. Fourteen C-130 Hercules transports had also escaped to Thailand and Singapore and four of these also arrived at MASDC in 1976.

Almost seventy USAF C-118 Liftmasters were retired to MASDC in 1975. Most of them were sold the next year to civilian operators, although a few were transferred to the Navy. The Liftmaster was the first Military Airlift Command aircraft to fly the Atlantic non-stop. In 1964 they were added to MAC aeromedical evacuation units in the United States. They were used

in Europe and the Pacific, including Vietnam, for evacuation of patients from combat areas and from theatre points of pick-up. Their replacement is the jet-equipped C-9 Nightingale, the military version of the DC-9 airliner.

The last C-119 'Flying Boxcars' were retired by the Air Force and Marine Corps in 1975. The majority had been sold for scrap by 1979, although five remained in the RIT area of AMARC until quite recently. Many C-119Gs were converted to AC-119G Shadow and AC-119K Stinger gunships and used in Vietnam. (Readers may like to read the author's book *Any Time, Any Place* published by Airlife and the Naval Institute Press in 1994 for the story of the Stingers' and Shadows' service in Vietnam.)

The Navy's A-6B Intruder appeared at MASDC in July 1975, when two were processed in from Attack Squadron 34. They remained for three years until they were flown out for conversion to A-6Es and eventual return to service. Since then many other A-6s have come and gone from both Navy and Marine units.

Surplus Air Force and Army utility aircraft were offered for sale in large numbers from 1975 onwards and nearly all took up civilian registrations. These included fifty short take-off and landing (STOL) U-10 Couriers and 200 U-6A Beavers.

Supplies of aircraft to friendly governments continued during 1975 and a score of T-33s and six F-104s were withdrawn from storage and flown to Taiwan to join the Chinese Nationalist Air Force. This continued into 1976, when the 27 A-37B Dragonflies that had survived the fall of South Vietnam were supplied to South Korea. They were supplemented in 1977 by six C-123 Provider transport aircraft, retired earlier by the Alaskan Air National Guard.

Several large aircraft sales took place in 1976, consisting mainly of reclaimed fighters and bombers. The Navy no longer had any use for its TF-8A Crusader training aircraft and Consolidated Aeronautics, a local scrapyard, purchased fifty of them. The Sun Valley Aviation Company of Phoenix purchased some 150 Navy TF-9 Cougar fighters and 25 EB-66 Destroyers. The latter were light tactical bombers, modified by the Air Force and used extensively over North Vietnam by their Electronic Warfare squadrons. Sun Valley Aviation also purchased a handful of derelict F-102s and obtained 100 more in 1977.

The B-58 Hustler bombers which had been in storage since 1970 came under the hammer in 1977 and all 82 were purchased by Southwestern Alloys. They were towed across to their yard just outside the perimeter fence of MASDC, broken up and melted down into ingots in their furnace.

Sixty HH-43F Huskie helicopters were purchased by Allied Aircraft in 1977. It was the first helicopter used by the Air Force especially for airborne fire-fighting and crash-rescue operations. Allied had also bought two dozen OH-43D Marine Corps versions five years earlier. One of each are currently on display at the nearby Pima Air Museum.

The year 1977 also saw an upgrading of the centre's processes for examining reclaimed parts. It is necessary to be able to determine which spare parts are serviceable for re-use from among those that are damaged or worn out. The two inspection processes then in use were a liquid penetrant test and a magnetic particle inspection. The liquid penetrant examination of aircraft parts was carried out by placing the part in a dye bath, which would reveal cracks inside the item when the part was exposed to a black light. This process was used for parts composed of aluminium, stainless steel and other materials which cannot be magnetised. Parts composed of metals which could be magnetised were subjected to magnetic particle inspection. The part to be inspected would be coated with powdered steel shavings mixed with kerosene and when it was exposed to black light the cracks would show up as lines.

Three new processes were then introduced: X-ray inspection, ultrasonic inspection and eddy current inspection. The X-ray machine used to inspect aircraft parts was much more powerful, at 150,000 volts, than medical machines. In the ultrasonic inspection, fluid was put on the part and high frequency sound waves sent through the item registered pulses on a scope, to indicate whether or not there was a flaw in it. Lastly, the eddy current technique was used by measuring the pattern of flow of an electric current thrust into the part.

By the end of 1977 1,424 aircraft were waiting reclamation, the largest number being 171 Navy T-33s; 523 aircraft were awaiting sale, transfer or donation to appropriate agencies and 2,355 aircraft and helicopters were in storage. Times had changed, though, and the majority of the stored aircraft – 1,108 – belonged to the Navy, with 678 Air Force, 563 Army and six Coast Guard. Amongst the Navy aircraft to arrive in 1977 were seven S-3A Vikings. The S-3 was taking over the anti-submarine search and strike role from the S-2 Tracker, and 161 of the latter were in long-term storage, with another 116 undergoing reclamation at the end of the year.

In 1978 Strategic Air Command retired sixty of its older B-52 D and F models to MASDC. At the same time the Texas Air National Guard retired the last KC-97Ls from service. Over 600 of the type had been retired to MASDC over the years. They have proved surprisingly popular in the aircraft sales, despite the government requirement that the purchaser remove the refuelling boom and pumps from the fuel tanker versions.

Helicopter sales resumed in 1978 with the first of 300 obsolete TH-55A trainers being put out to tender. Foreign military sales also continued with 35 F-8H Crusaders going to the Philippine Air Force.

One of the more interesting types of aircraft to arrive in 1979 was the EB-57E Canberra, retired by the 17th Defense Systems Evaluation Squadron at Malmstrom AFB, Montana. They were equipped with the latest devices for jamming and penetrating air defences and were used to simulate an enemy bomber force, attempting to find gaps in the air defence systems. The final examples of the EB-57 were retired by the 134th DSES, Vermont ANG, in 1982.

Boeing and McDonnell-Douglas both fielded two prototype aircraft for the Advanced Medium STOL Transport (AMST) competition in the early 1970s. Both types underwent testing and evaluation at Edwards AFB by the manufacturers and Air Force Systems Command officials. The programme was suspended in 1979 following the withdrawal of Air Force funding, and the two McDonnell-Douglas YC-15As arrived at MASDC in August 1979, followed by the two Boeing YC-14As in April 1980. One of each type has been loaned to the Pima Air Museum on the condition that they be returned at 24 hours' notice if required.

The Air Force Reserve began to retire its C-123K Providers in June 1980 and some have since appeared on the civil market, in the colours of one of the fire-bomber companies. Two or three others have been withdrawn from storage, allegedly for use by certain government agencies for tasks involving clandestine flights to South American countries. Examples have even been seized by the Drugs Enforcement Agency; apparently the type has potential for use by drug runners.

The phase-out of the F-105 Thunderchief also began in the summer of 1980 when the 35th TFW at George AFB, California replaced its F-105G Wild Weasels with the F-4G. There were still a couple of years to go before the last would retire, having given stalwart service for over two decades, including the years of war in south-east Asia from which 397 of them did not return.

Visitors to MASDC in September 1981

had to blink and look again at the sight of seventeen American Airlines Boeing 707s parked on the arrival ramp. They were the first of over 130 civilian Boeing 707s purchased by the Air Force, including the bulk of the Trans World Airlines fleet. All were being preserved in storage, after the removal of their engines and vertical and horizontal stabilisers, for future use by the KC-135 tanker fleet. The commercial carriers could no longer operate the Boeing 707s economically and the Air Force bought them for between $500,000 and $1 million each. Spare parts worth many times that amount have been removed from each aircraft.

On 12 January 1982 the first F-106A Delta Dart arrived for storage from the 48th Fighter Interceptor Squadron. Over 100 had arrived by December 1985 when it was announced that, under an Air Force programme called 'Pacer Six', about 200 F-106s would be converted to drones and used as aerial targets by the Air Force and Army. The Air Force began replacing the F-106s with the F-15 Eagle and earmarked the Delta Dart as a replacement for the PQM-102 and QF-100 drones. Tactical Air Command planned to use the new drones until 1995 and then replace them with F-4 Phantom drones, following that type's retirement from service.

As a follow-on to the 'Pave Deuce' F-102 drone conversion programme, Sperry's Defense and Space Systems Division began converting the first of eighty F-100 Super Sabres to QF-100 drones in 1983. In addition, Flight Systems Incorporated at Mojave, California commenced the conversion of 209 more.

Sales of Navy aircraft have done rather well in recent years, with eighty S-2 Trackers and 48 E-1 Tracers – the latter an airborne early warning version of the S-2 being sold to Consolidated Aeronautics in Tucson. Although all had suffered spare parts reclamation, they were offered for sale as potentially flyable. Despite the fact that one or two S-2s have been acquired by warbird enthusiasts, the only current commercial market for them is the fire-bomber operators. A large number of S-2s are already in service with the California Division of Forestry and their counterparts in Canada and France. A number of South American countries have also taken an interest in MASDC's stocks of surplus S-2s. In 1981 Grumman overhauled and supplied Trackers to Brazil and then in 1982 to Uruguay. More recently they have done the same with S-2s destined for the Peruvian Navy.

Douglas A-4 Skyhawk stocks at MASDC were reduced by around 100 in 1983. Allied Aircraft won a contract to crate and ship sixteen TA-4Bs to Singapore, who had received an initial batch of A-4Cs in 1980.

Eighty-eight more were removed to an overhaul facility where forty complete examples were to be made for the Air Force of Malaysia.

The summer of 1983 also saw fifteen ex-Navy F-4J Phantoms fly out for overhaul, prior to dispatch to England to add another Phantom squadron to the Royal Air Force. This reinforced the RAF Phantom strength, spread thin by the need to maintain a squadron at operational readiness on the Falkland Islands.

Portugal was next on the list to receive surplus Navy aircraft. Thirty A-7s were crated and sent to the Vought Corporation's factory in Dallas for modification into 24 A-7Ps and six TA-7Ps.

As fast as the Navy reduced their inventory at MASDC, more aircraft arrived to increase it again. From 1983 onwards more A-7s were retired, together with over 250 Navy and Marine Phantoms. Over two dozen early model P-3A Orion patrol aircraft arrived for storage. Some were earmarked for transfer to the Customs Service, while reclamation has already begun on others.

The Air Force had also been busy and forty B-52s were sold for scrap, leaving around 230 others still in storage. As a part of the Strategic Arms Limitation Talks the B-52s have to be dismembered and left for 120 days so that Soviet Satellites can verify their destruction.

In 1984 the Air Force also found a use for two of the DC-130 Hercules transports which had been used to launch remote-controlled drones in Vietnam and retired in 1979. The Aeronautical Systems Division's 4950th Test Wing at Wright-Patterson AFB requested them for use as testbed aircraft for new electronic components. The idea saved the Air Force about $28 million, the basic price of two new C-130s.

Over the decade following the United States' withdrawal from south-east Asia, the wheel had turned full circle. The old obsolete types had largely gone and those that were left were providing their worth as spare parts 'banks'. The numbers of aircraft arriving for storage were slowing down due to a trend in the armed forces of retaining their aircraft longer. New aircraft are expensive to build and repair, so the spare parts bank at MASDC had become more valuable. The success of the centre was reflected in its balance sheets. For every dollar spent on its upkeep in 1984, MASDC was able to return to the government $13.18.

Retired by Navy Observation Squadron VO-67 following duties involving the dropping of people/vehicle sensors over enemy infiltration routes in Laos, Lockheed OP-2E Neptune *131525* was sold for scrap in 1975. *(Author's Collection)*

(RIGHT)
Many Republic F-105 Thunderchiefs were noted with various types of fuselage artwork during the author's visit in April 1984. *(Philip Chinnery)*

(BELOW)
A line of Republic F-105 Thunderchiefs stretching into the distance in April 1984, with Wild Weasel F-105G *63-300* nearest.
(Philip Chinnery)

A row of Convair F-102A Delta Daggers, with *57-0852*/FJ2260 from the 134th Fighter Interceptor Squadron, Vermont Air National Guard nearest the camera. Retired in 1974, it left in 1981 for conversion to PQM-102B target drone. *(Philip Chinnery)*

McDonnell F-101B Voodoo *57-0282* was retired by the 136th Fighter Interceptor Squadron, New York Air National Guard in October 1978 and was loaned to the Pima Air Museum in 1979 where it remains today.

(Author's Collection)

(LEFT)
These short take-off and landing (STOL) Helio U-10A Super Couriers were originally purchased for Air America to use in Laos during the Vietnam war. These former West Virginia Air National Guard models are destined for civilian owners in late 1978. *(Author's Collection)*

(BELOW)
A row of North American T-2B Buckeye Navy trainer aircraft photographed in October 1978 with *155233*, formerly with Navy Training Squadron VT-10 nearest. It went back into Navy service in February 1982 and returned to the boneyard for the last time in 1991. *(Author's Collection)*

Storm clouds in the background contrast with the camouflage of Republic F-84F Thunderstreak *51-1772* when photographed in November 1978, seven years after retirement from the 101st Tactical Fighter Squadron, Massachusetts Air National Guard. *(Author's Collection)*

(ABOVE)
One of the last Curtiss C-46D Commandos at MASDC. *44-77614* served with the 733rd Troop Carrier Wing until retirement in May 1958. It was sold to Southwest Alloys in Tucson in 1979, the year after this photograph was taken.
(Author's Collection)

(LEFT)
De Havilland Canada YC-7A Caribou *57-3081* wearing red and white Army markings in 1978 was severely damaged in a storm five years later and was scrapped around 1990.
(Author's Collection)

(ABOVE)
The 58th Weather Reconnaissance Squadron at Kirtland Air Force Base, New Mexico operated the Martin WB-57F Canberra before the last models were sent for storage. Note the large engines and wings on *63-13302*, still in storage after twenty years on behalf of the Air Force Museum.
(Author's Collection)

(RIGHT)
The desert sand had made little impression on the colourful markings on these Vought F-8K Crusaders, still preserved in storage in January 1982. *145583* served with Navy Fighter Squadron VF-302 before retirement in 1973. *(Philip Chinnery)*

(LEFT)
Douglas C-54T Skymaster *90411* was photographed in October 1978 wearing the markings of the Fleet Marine Force Atlantic. It was sold in July 1980 to a civilian operator in California. Note the Curtiss C-46 Commandos in the background.
(Author's Collection)

(BELOW)
Douglas A-4C Skyhawk *147814* was retired by Marines Attack Squadron VMA-134 in July 1973. The Reserve unit now flies the F/A-18A Hornet.
(Author's Collection)

(ABOVE)
Douglas NB-66A Destroyer *53-0488* arrived at MASDC after service with the Air Research and Development Centre in June 1974 and was sold for scrap in November 1976.
(Patrick Martin/Ben Knowles)

(RIGHT)
North American F-100F Super Sabre *56-3972* arrived in June 1973 and departed in July 1981 for the Ogden Air Logistics Center at Hill Air Force Base, Utah. Note the Air Force Systems Command badge.
(Author's Collection)

(Douglas KC-97L Stratotanker *52-0869 Salt Lake City* was retired by the Utah Air National Guard in December 1977 and scrapped in 1983. *(Philip Chinnery)*

A line of North American RA-5C
Vigilante reconnaissance aircraft in
storage in March 1974. *151726*,
nearest, used to serve on the aircraft
carrier *John F. Kennedy* with Navy
Reconnaissance Attack Squadron
RVAH-14 until retirement in 1971.
(Author's Collection)

(LEFT)
McDonnell Douglas YC-15A *72-1876* has been in storage since 1979. It was a contender for the advanced medium STOL competition and was stored after funding was withdrawn, together with *72-1875* which is on loan to the Pima Air Museum. Note the field of C-130s in the background. *(Philip Chinnery)*

(BELOW)
Seen on the arrival ramp in February 1974 this Air Force Rescue Bell UH-1F Iroquis *63-13148* has already had its inventory number 4HF062 painted on its nose. *(Author's Collection)*

Douglas C-133 Cargomasters in storage in 1971. The nearest, C-133A *54-0137* from the 436th Military Airlift Wing, arrived on 7th January and was scrapped with the bulk of the fleet early in 1974. *(Henry F. Carter)*

Photographed on the departure ramp in September 1988, former Indiana Air National Guard QF-100D Super Sabre *55-3741* can be identified as a radio-controlled drone aircraft by its red nose, wingtips and tail assembly. *(Philip Chinnery)*

AMARC AND INTO THE 90s

The Air Force decided to attempt to change MASDC's 'aircraft boneyard' image in 1985 and renamed the centre the Aerospace Maintenance and Regeneration Center (AMARC). This change also reflected an addition to the workload of the centre with the development of an aircraft contingency withdrawal programme. This was designed to supply the armed forces in a national emergency with mission-capable aircraft on short notice.

During the fiscal year 1985 $301 million worth of spare parts were returned to military warehouses, an increase of 74 per cent over FY84, and 173 aircraft were reclaimed for spare parts, an increase of 49 per cent over the previous year. Because of the increased re-utilisation of parts and aircraft, particularly in the form of target drones, the financial return to the government doubled to $26.54 for each dollar spent.

In late September 1985 one aircraft burst into life after nine years in storage when a Lockheed EC-121K Super Constellation restoration project was completed by the locally based 41st Electronic Combat Squadron. 'Project Warrior' involved the reconditioning of the aircraft for a flight to Tinker Air Force Base to complete their collection of airborne early warning and control planes. A different generation of aircraft were heading in the opposite direction as the Marine Corps began to retire some of its AV-8A and C Harrier vertical take-off aircraft in late 1985. The first arrived in August and over the next three years forty more would follow.

The newly-named centre still continues its traditional mission of storage and 1986 saw the arrival of the last C-123s and O-2s in the Air Force inventory, together with over 100 T-39 Sabreliners. The last C-123, serial number *55-4547*, was a UC-123K, one configured for aerial spraying, and it was piloted by Major-General Sloan R. Gill, chief of the Air Force Reserves. The last O-2 arrived from the 21st Tactical Air Support Squadron and was built by Cessna as a replacement for the 0-1 'Bird Dog', used as forward air control aircraft during the Vietnam war.

The Coast Guard began making more use of the centre and put ten of their HC-130Bs into storage, so that the engines could be removed and fitted to new replacement HC-130s as a cost-saving measure. They were also joined by at least twenty-two Coast Guard HH-52A helicopters.

The Air Force KC-135 Stratotanker refurbishment programme was well under way, with 116 out of an estimated 200 civilian models purchased by the Air Force. Their engines were removed and fitted to the Air Force models, together with the airline seats, galleys, carpets and drapes. The new turbofan engines are more powerful, less noisy, less smoky and cheaper to operate. One complete cockpit assembly was donated to the Museum of Science and Technology in Tucson's sister city, Guadalajara, Mexico.

Battle Damage Repair Training is another area in which obsolete aircraft can play their part. Surplus Phantoms, Thunderchiefs and others began to depart from AMARC for repair units in Holland, England, Germany and bases throughout the States. The aircraft are shot full of holes to simulate combat damage and are then repaired by the BDR troops, who splice new wires, make new hydraulic pipes and eventually restore the aircraft to flying shape.

Aircraft impounded by the Customs Service were also being stored at AMARC, and up to fifty small aircraft were present around this time. In addition, a Boeing 707 was parked nearby, having been seized in Galveston, Texas, loaded with mortars, machine-guns and other contraband weapons destined for Central America.

Approximately 90 Air Force Phantoms were retired between 1987 and 1988, although the total soon dropped to 68 F-4C and D models suggesting that, for some, their stay was brief. The AMARC transportation branch was busy during 1987, with a Navy F-14 shipped out by Super Guppy to Pomona, California; Navy A-7s crated for overland shipment to Jacksonville, Florida; Navy F-8 Crusaders prepared for rail shipment to Dallas, Texas; and even a C-130 Hercules prepared for towing overland by truck. Spare parts reclamation was proceeding well and during the year 114,000 parts valued at $72 million were removed and returned to Department of Defense stocks.

It was announced that AMARC would be used to destroy ground-launched cruise missiles under the terms of the Intermediate-Range Nuclear Forces (INF) Treaty. 429 Air Force Cruise missiles and more than 100 Army Pershing 2 missiles were to be destroyed. The missile warheads will be removed before the missiles arrive at AMARC and the fuel, worth 14 dollars a gallon, will also be removed and re-used. The guidance set and jet engine are to be saved and can be re-used in the Navy's Tomahawk sea-launched cruise missiles. The missiles and their transporter-erector launchers will then be destroyed by cutting the weapons in half lengthwise, while a Soviet verification team watches the process.

AMARC also began storing production tooling for types of aircraft no longer in production, such as the A-10 ground attack aircraft and the B-1 bomber. Should the need arise to re-manufacture any component, the tooling can be located and shipped to a contractor. The tooling is coated with a product called Pro Cote 129, which is similar in appearance to clear varnish and should preserve the tooling for five to seven years.

One typical aircraft sale took place on 12 January 1988 when the Defense Re-utilisation and Marketing Service offered seven Boeing 707s and 22 Bell UH-1 'Huey' helicopters for sale by tender. All were sold for scrap and the aircraft soon left for scrapyards surrounding the base. Bob Hoover's company AMCEP purchased a number of surplus Boeing 707s and Lockheed SP-2H Neptunes around this time and stored them in Bob's Airpark, just outside the perimeter of the base.

The oldest US Army Bell UH-1 'Iroquois', or 'Huey' as it is universally called, was retired to AMARC on 13 September 1988. The retirement ceremony marked the start of a massive programme to retire approximately 6,000 Army aircraft over the following twenty years. Amongst the first to retire was almost two-thirds of the UH-1 fleet, in order to make room for newer acquisitions such as the Blackhawk and Apache. With more than 3,400 Hueys in its inventory, the retirement of some 2,300 of them began in earnest towards the end of 1988. The majority will not stay long. Many will be scrapped or sold and some given to civil authorities.

The number of aircraft in storage had been reduced to 2,600 prior to the start of the Army withdrawal programme. With the centre occupying 2,262 acres there was plenty of room to spare.

One office at AMARC that receives little publicity is the Navy Field Service Office, a detachment of Naval Air Systems Command with half a dozen people providing administrative, logistical and technical support for the transfer of Navy aircraft from Air Systems Command to AMARC. Towards the end of 1990 they were preparing for an influx of Grumman F-14 Tomcat fighter aircraft, following the reduction of tension in Eastern Europe and budgetary restraints leading to the reduction of the size of the squadrons. Another project was monitoring the use of vinyl bags to cover some of the Navy's Phantoms, instead of using the traditional 'Spraylat'. The bags cost $6,500 each, against more than $26,000 to process-in and maintain an F-4 for four years.

The processing of aircraft into storage has changed since the early days of the B-29s, but is no less complex a procedure. On arrival all explosives, such as ejection seat charges, are removed, together with any pilferable or particularly valuable items. The aircraft is then washed to remove industrial or marine residues and inspected for corrosion. Navy aircraft, especially those on aircraft carriers, have been exposed to corrosive salt air and require anti-corrosion treatment. The aircraft is then towed to the Preservation Section. On the process-in or flush farm, line mechanics drain the engines and hydraulic lines of oil. They also drain and reclaim the fuel from the aircraft and then pump in a lightweight oil, which is again drained, leaving a protective oil film in the lines and tanks to protect them from drying out or corroding. Engine intakes and exhausts are then covered with paper and any seams, inspection hatches, openings and rubber seals in the upper half of the aircraft are taped. The paper tape and any fragile surfaces such as canopies and radomes are then sprayed with a heavy plastic-like material called 'Spraylat', first with a coat of black and then with white to reflect sunlight. Wheel-wells, drainage holes and other openings under the aircraft remain open to allow circulation of air to minimise condensation.

Apart from protecting the aircraft from dust, sand and the elements, the main purpose of the 'Spraylat' is to maintain the internal temperature of the aircraft at about ten to fifteen degrees hotter than the surrounding air. Without such protection the inside of an aircraft could reach 200°F, causing damage to rubber parts and functional components. Unlike the B-29 cocoon, the 'Spraylat' can be easily peeled off should the aircraft be required to fly again.

Once the preservation process is completed the aircraft is moved into the desert. Ninety days later it is inspected again to ensure the preservative is still intact, then once every 180 days until the aircraft has been stored for four years. At that time the aircraft is de-preserved and all systems are inspected to make sure there has been no damage.

This method of preservation is currently undergoing evaluation and AMARC has two full-time engineers in its desert laboratory undertaking research in aircraft preservation. Tedlar tape is now being used, which does not require the usual 'Spraylat' coating, and a saving of seven man hours and $620 per aircraft is the result. Experiments have been carried out with new aircraft covers for aircraft with a high probability of withdrawal, and the savings in tape and 'Spraylat' could, in the case of the F-4, amount to $1,400 per year.

As AMARC looked towards the 1990s, what was on the horizon? They were on the threshold of a whole new era, with defence budgets shrinking and arms agreements dictating new, lower force levels. Rough estimates of aircraft arrivals were 650 in 1990 and 400 in 1991. However, with squadrons of F-111s earmarked for retirement, 400 Phantoms looking for a new home, plus more B-52s, P-3s, A-7s and C-130s due to retire, the influx of new arrivals is expected to increase dramatically.

The Base Closure and Realignment Act passed by Congress in 1988 and the planned reorganisation of the major USAF Commands signed the death warrant for many squadrons. Plans were under way to deactivate Military Airlift Command, Tactical Air Command and Strategic Air Command and replace them with Air Mobility Command and Air Combat Command. AMARC would report direct to Air Force Materiel Command, established on 1 July 1992 at Wright-Patterson AFB, Ohio.

What effect would all this have on AMARC? In August 1993, eleven years after his first visit, the author decided to go and see.

These Bell OH-58A Kiowa helicopters are fitted with a device on the cabin roof designed to cut any cables or wires that may snag the rotor blades whilst flying low. XE022 is *68-16854* which arrived in 1988. *(Philip Chinnery)*

(LEFT)
Marines Fairchild C-119F Flying Boxcar *131699* was sold for scrap to Dross Metals of Tucson in October 1980 after eight years in storage.
(Author's Collection)

(BELOW)
Navy Lockheed EC-121K Constellation *143184* served with Navy Airborne Early Warning Training Unit Atlantic (*AEWTULANT*) before arrival at MASDC early in 1966. It spent only a couple of months in storage before being transferred to the Air Force.
(Philip Chinnery)

After only four years in storage, former Navy Douglas C-117D Skytrooper *138820* was photographed on the departure ramp in September 1981, preparing for its flight to join its new owner in California. *(Philip Chinnery)*

(ABOVE)
The Southwest Alloys scrapyard, just across the road from AMARC. The yard was full of Convair T-29 Samaritans when this photograph was taken in June 1984. *(Philip Chinnery)*

(LEFT)
Note the unusual lumps and bumps on this Convair EC-131G Samaritan *141024* following its retirement from the Pacific Missile Test Center in November 1979. *(Philip Chinnery)*

A view across the 'elephants graveyard' of B-52s towards B-52F *57-0060*
which arrived in 1971.
(*Author's Collection*)

The first Sikorsky CH-54A Tarhe 'Flying Crane' to be stored at AMARC. Parked on Celebrity Row, note the fields of Phantoms in the background and the Starlifter tails in the distance. *(Philip Chinnery)*

(ABOVE)
Convair Country. C-131D Samaritan *54-2814* wearing inventory number CS087 arrived in 1987 and is still being held for the Air Force Museum.
(Philip Chinnery)

(RIGHT)
After eighteen years in storage, prototype Boeing 707-80 *N70700* is prepared for return to the manufacturer in 1990. Because no jack pads were in existence to fit the aircraft, they could not test the landing gear and had to fly the aircraft to Seattle with the gear down.
(Andy Anderson)

Retired by the New Jersey Air National Guard, the last unit to fly the Convair F-106A Delta Dart, *59-0043*/FN194 was covered in artwork that the AMARC employees tried hard to preserve intact. *(Andy Anderson)*

(RIGHT)
Shown in its shipboard pose with folded wings, the aft fuselage of this Navy Grumman C-1A Trader had been removed when photographed in March 1988. *(Philip Chinnery)*

(BELOW)
The one and only Coast Guard Aerospatiale HH-65A Dauphin at AMARC in March 1988. Parked on 'Celebrity Row' and completely covered with 'Spraylat', its inventory number is 47 001 and Coast Guard serial number 6509. It has since been returned to the Coast Guard.
(Philip Chinnery)

(ABOVE)
Newly-arrived Marines Bell AH-1J Sea Cobras *157773*/7H182 and *157757*/7H183 were photographed in March 1988. Only the engine intakes have been sealed so far. *(Philip Chinnery)*

(LEFT)
Seen in the RIT area in March 1988, Army YC-7A Caribou *57-3081*, Navy P-3A Orion *151351* and Air Force F-104D Starfighter *57-1320*. All have since been sold for scrap.

(Philip Chinnery)

(RIGHT)
This North American F-100 Super Sabre is undergoing extensive maintenance prior to departure to the Sperry Corporation for conversion to a target drone. *(Philip Chinnery)*

(BELOW)
Fairchild Republic T-46A trainer *84-0493* arrived for storage in 1987 with *85-1596*. Both are still currently in storage on 'Celebrity Row'. The T-46 was designed as a possible replacement for the Cessna T-37 trainer. *(Philip Chinnery)*

Douglas C-118A Liftmaster *CG029* is former Air Force Logistics Command *53-3298*, which arrived in February 1975 and is still in storage today.

(Philip Chinnery)

Douglas C-118A Liftmaster *53-3239*
arrived in June 1975 and is still
present in the RIT area. *(Philip Chinnery)*

(ABOVE)
This row contains the 29 Bell TH-57A Sea Rangers in storage during the author's visit in March 1988. *157355* is nearest the camera, wearing the inventory number 4H001.
(Philip Chinnery)

(LEFT)
A line of Boeing CH-47A Chinook helicopters in storage in March 1988 with *62-2131* nearest. They have since all returned to service. *(Philip Chinnery)*

Boeing NB-52E Stratofortress *56-0632* arrived for storage in June 1974 after use by Boeing and the Air Force Flight Dynamics Laboratory for Control Configured Vehicle tests. Since this picture was taken in 1988 it has been used for explosive tests and the port rear fuselage has been extensively damaged. Perhaps retirement to a museum would have been more appropriate. *(Philip Chinnery)*

The effect on an aircraft's centre of gravity after the removal of its engines is clearly shown by Navy Lockheed DC-130A Hercules *158228* which has been in storage since retirement from Navy Composite Squadron VC-3 in 1979. *(Philip Chinnery)*

Over 500 Hughes TH-55A Osage primary training helicopters were retired by the Army between 1971 and 1974. The majority were given to local government agencies, colleges and the Royal Thai Army. These were photographed in 1984, but none remain at AMARC today.
(Philip Chinnery)

(ABOVE)
The remains of a Coast Guard Lockheed HC-130B Hercules in the RIT area. All Coast Guard Hercules aircraft at AMARC are now carried on the Air Force inventory.
(Philip Chinnery)

(LEFT)
Grumman E-1B Tracer *148130* served with Navy Airborne Early Warning Squadron VAW-111 on the aircraft carrier USS *Ranger* before retirement in 1973. It was later sold with many others to Consolidated Aeronautics of Tucson. *(Philip Chinnery)*

(ABOVE)
The red star indicates that this McDonnell F-5 Phantom shot down a North Vietnamese MiG fighter during the Vietnam war. A former resident of AMARC, the aircraft is on loan to the Pima Air Museum. *(Philip Chinnery)*

(Right)
'Abundance of Strength' badge on one of the silver B-52s that have been in storage since the 1960s. *(Philip Chinnery)*

(LEFT)
A shot near sundown of the Pima Air Museum's latest B-52 with 'Valkyrie' nose art and 'Libertatem Defendimus' badge of the 2nd Bomb Wing. Note anti-flash curtains in cockpit, used to protect the crew during explosion of nuclear bombs. *(Philip Chinnery)*

(BELOW)
A jet-assisted Fairchild C-119C Flying Boxcar, N13743 was donated to the Pima Air Museum by Hemet Valley Flying Service. Formerly 49-0132 it was stored at MASDC until the early 1970s when it left for a new career as a fire-bomber. *(Philip Chinnery)*

Long lines of McDonnell F-4 Phantoms at AMARC, with *65-0793* formerly with the 171st Fighter Squadron, Michigan Air National Guard nearest. The aircraft arrived in March 1990 after the unit converted to the F-16. *(Philip Chinnery)*

(LEFT)
Fairchild A-10A Thunderbolt II AC008/*79-0224* with 'Have Gun Will Travel' nose art, saw action during the Gulf War with the 511th Tactical Fighter Squadron, 10th TFW, based at RAF Alconbury, England and arrived in January 1992. *(Philip Chinnery)*

(BELOW)
McDonnell Douglas AV-8A Harrier 7A008/*159371* with its refuelling probe extended, heads a line of the type behind a row of Air Force Phantoms. It has been in storage since January 1986. *(Philip Chinnery)*

Relative newcomers to AMARC, these
McDonnell Douglas F-15A Eagle
fighters began to arrive for storage in
1991. *74-0134* nearest arrived in May
1992. *(Philip Chinnery)*

(ABOVE)
A McDonnell F-4 Phantom trying out the new plastic bag method of storage, designed to save on the costs of preserving the aircraft with Spraylat.
(Philip Chinnery)

(LEFT)
A line of Air Force Vought A-7 aircraft with two-seater A-7K *79-0462*/AE195 nearest. The small pod under the air intake housed the LANA (Low Altitude Night Attack) system, incorporating AN/AAR-49 FLIR (Forward Looking Infra-Red)
(Philip Chinnery)

(RIGHT)
Fairchild C-123K Provider *54-0689* served with the 302nd Tactical Airlift Wing, Air Force Reserve and was photographed on the fuel removal ramp in September 1980.
(Author's Collection)

(BELOW)
Another resident of the RIT area, General Dynamics F-111A *63-9777* was used by NASA until it was stored as a source of spare parts in 1971.
(Philip Chinnery)

A former Navy Grumman S-2 Tracker anti-submarine aircraft in Bob's Airpark, a salvage yard just outside AMARC. Note the C-130 coming in to land in the distance. *(Philip Chinnery)*

One rare and unusual arrival in 1989
was Navy ZPG-3W airship *144243*
seen together with T/Sgt Marc Brazil,
one of the dedicated tour guides.
(Philip Chinnery)

(ABOVE)
These Sikorsky CH-37C Mojave helicopters did not remain in MASDC long after retirement in 1966. These were photographed in the Allied Aircraft salvage yard in 1982. Note the large clamshell access doors below the cockpit. *(Philip Chinnery)*

(LEFT)
Parked in its shipboard pose with folded wings, Grumman US-2B Tracker *136643* served at Alameda Naval Air Station, California until December 1978 and was photographed in storage ten years later.
(Philip Chinnery)

(ABOVE)
Grumman E-2B Hawkeye 2E003/
151716 had undergone extensive spare
parts reclamation when photographed
in March 1988. Its radome lies behind
on wooden supports. It was retired in
1982 and is still in storage today.
(Philip Chinnery)

(RIGHT)
Army Grumman OV-1C Mohawk
0-18884 was flown by the Georgia Air
National Guard prior to storage and
display on AMARC's Celebrity Row in
1988. The aircraft is used in the
battlefield surveillance role and later
models took part in Operation Desert
Storm. *(Philip Chinnery)*

Photographed on the departure ramp in June 1984, Marine Corps Sikorsky VH-3A Sea King *148037*/9H001 has been in storage since 1976 and is returning to service with VIP duties squadron HMX-1. *(Philip Chinnery)*

Foreign markings in this row of
Lockheed P-3 Orions. 2P070 is P-3A
150507 awaiting transfer to the
Chilean Navy along with half a dozen
others at the end of 1993.

(Philip Chinnery)

END OF THE COLD WAR

It was 112 degrees Fahrenheit in the shade. Damn hot, even for Tucson. And as for shade, all that I could find was under the drooping wing of B-52D Stratofortress *56-0580*, a resident in the boneyard for over a decade. I did not have to go far to find some shade, as there were 326 other B-52s around me to choose from.

I had visited the centre half a dozen times since 1982, the last time in 1990. Now, however, everything had changed. AMARC currently employs over 700 civilians, almost 300 more than my first visit, and currently stores almost 4,400 aircraft on its 2,712 acres, eighty-five per cent of which remain airworthy. Roughly 100 aircraft are arriving each month, caused by the reduction in the size of the armed forces following the collapse of the Soviet Union. It marks the largest influx since the end of the Vietnam war.

About a third of the aircraft to arrive at AMARC will eventually depart, to return to service or by transfer to other government agencies or foreign governments. Recently, some Cessna 0-2 Skymasters, former Air Force forward air control aircraft, were shipped to Zimbabwe and the Ivory Coast to be used in the war against big game poachers. Six North American OV-10A Bronco aircraft departed in April 1993 for the forestry service and T-38Bs are being sent back to Holloman AFB to train Nationalist Chinese who are purchasing a quantity. A couple of Lockheed P-3 Orions had already departed for Chile, while others wait their turn, already painted in Chilean Naval markings. UP-3As *151384*, *150518*, *150607*, *152141* and *151354*, and P-3As *150507*, *152165* and *149677* are earmarked for Chile.

As of August 1993, some 4,424 aircraft are in storage, almost a thousand more than during my visit in 1982. Other items such as missiles, drones and aircraft awaiting processing bring the total inventory to 4,792. From these, 3,227 belong to the Air Force, 1,454 to the Navy and Marines, 73 to the Army and 38 to the Coast Guard.

On the day of my visit, despite the heat and the necessity to drink a gallon of water to combat dehydration, I managed to take some 400 photographs and there was plenty of choice of subjects. There are 1,088 Phantoms in storage at AMARC, 211 Navy, 877 Air Force and over 500 Navy and Air Force A-7s. Parked in long rows and displaying many types of tail markings and nose art, the aircraft are a photographer's dream. Some of their old adversaries, MiG fighters, have also arrived. Flown by the Navy Air Test Center at China Lake and now disassembled on pallets, half a dozen MiG-15s and -17s will surely be earmarked for museums. Two of each type have already found their way across the road to the Pima Air Museum, where they have been assembled and painted in different communist air force markings.

I was surprised to see some F-16s in storage. I would have been even more surprised if anyone had told me that there would be 107 in storage by March 1994! Around ten had been semi-preserved near the flight line, where their engines are run and systems checked regularly. Some have come straight from the factory, and when one aircraft was recently found to have a radar problem, General Dynamics was called in to rectify the fault under warranty! A half dozen F-16s from the 160th Fighter Squadron, Alabama Air National Guard had also just taxied on to the arrival ramp. The pilots climbed out of their cockpits and into an Air Force bus, leaving their aircraft in the hands of the AMARC civilian workforce. The aircraft will eventually be sold to Israel and Pakistan, when that country has signed the nuclear non-proliferation agreement.

The arriving aircraft are processed in the same way as thousands of others before them. The aircraft are made safe and ejection seat cartridges are removed and an inventory is taken of accountable equipment. The aircraft is then washed, and some Marine CH-53s were undergoing this process during my visit. After the next stop, where the fuel is drained and the systems preserved with a 10-10 weight oil, the arrivals head for the large reclamation shed for preservation with 'Spraylat'. Navy T-34 trainers, E-2 Hawkeye AEW aircraft and Sikorsky SH-2 helicopters were being treated during my visit and an Air Force OV-10 Bronco was being sprayed out in the open. As mentioned previously, AMARC is currently testing huge wraparound plastic bags on 48 different aircraft. It is certainly cheaper than the $24 a gallon 'Spraylat', but not so successful, with some of the bags starting to come apart at the seams.

Because of the cutbacks in the Air Force inventory, some of the 'big guys' have started to arrive. Eight C-141 Starlifters are already in storage and two others were awaiting processing. Sixty-seven EC and KC-135s were present, together with 72 Air Force C-130s. It would be interesting to see the first C-5 Galaxy arrive; how long would it take to process one of those into storage? The nose art on the KC-135s is well worth photographing.

It was a surprise to see around 50 Army M-60 tanks parked next to some P-3 Orions in the RIT area. Apparently they have since departed, some to Nellis AFB for use as ground targets and others to be converted to radio-controlled targets.

Familiar faces were to be found amongst the rows of aircraft, such as the F-111Es carrying the *UH* tail markings of the 20th Fighter Wing disbanded at RAF Upper Heyford in England, and the *LN* tail code of the 48th Fighter Wing F-111Es replaced at RAF Lakenheath by the F-15E. Almost 200 Fairchild A-10 Thunderbolt II tank busters were in storage, after being blooded not against Warsaw Pact tank columns in central Europe, but against Saddam Hussein's Republican Guard in Kuwait and Iraq.

One hundred and eleven civilian Boeing 707s were present in varying conditions. Each cost the Air Force $900,000 and about five million dollars worth of spare parts have been removed from each aircraft; so for an outlay of $99.9 million the Air Force saved $555 million . Most of the world's 707 fleet are ending their days at AMARC. Almost all of TWA's fleet have now moved on to the local scrapyards, although there are plenty of others still left in storage. Some are used by agencies such as the FBI and Delta Force, as well as the British and Australian SAS, to improve their anti-hijacking and aircraft disabling techniques. One 707 was recently blown completely in half during one explosive test and more are still arriving. Two Royal Jordanian Cargo aircraft and one from Florida West were amongst five recently given to the Air Force in exchange for one 'brand new' model. When the Jordanian aircraft arrived, they were found to contain civilians who had gone along for the ride. Lacking the required paperwork to enter the USA, they were detained by the local immigration officials for a while, until they could be returned whence they came. Some of the old Boeing 707s are to be modified, then equipped with the highly sensitive Joint Surveillance Target Attack Radar System, JSTARS, which was invaluable during the Gulf war. The two prototypes provided a real-time method of tracking armour and other military vehicles a hundred miles inside enemy territory.

Back in the good old days, AMARC used to run a once a month photographic tour, when enthusiasts could spend a morning being ferried around the lines of aircraft to take photographs. Taxpayers could also take the kids along to see what the Air Force was doing with their money. Allegedly, a lack of tour guides and a misguided policy change along the lines of 'So what benefit is it to the Air Force to run these tours?' led to their demise. Now there is only a short tour on Mondays and Wednesdays and the passengers cannot leave the bus to take photographs. A great shame.

One of the first stops on the tour is

'Celebrity Row', where two dozen one-off and interesting aircraft are displayed. The most spectacular aircraft currently present is NASA 940, a huge 'Super Guppy', based on the C-97J Stratocruiser with C-133 engines, which dwarfs everything around it. NASA wants the centre to put more powerful C-130 engines on the aircraft so it can fly again. One 'Super Guppy' will replace two C-5s used to transport Atlas and Titan rocket boosters.

United Airlines have a Boeing 727, *N7004U*, in the row pending movement to a museum, and an Air Force example is parked nearby. Recently an Air Force F-4 MiG killer was replaced by RF-4C *65-0843* with its magnificent markings celebrating the 75th Anniversary of the 106th Recce Squadron of the Alabama ANG. A new type of helicopter has come to AMARC is parked on the row, a CH-54A Tarhe 'Flying Crane' *67-18415*. This unique helicopter has a position behind the pilots, facing aft, where a third pilot would sit to control the aircraft whilst picking up a cargo load with the giant hook. A second CH-54 is outside the entrance to the Pima Air Museum. A single USCG HU-25A Guardian, *2127*, is also parked on 'Celebrity Row'.

At present a further 300 acres of scrubland are being cleared to handle future arrivals. B-52G *57-6488*, carrying the tail code *LZ*, from the 42nd Bomb Wing at Loring AFB, Maine had just arrived to join the 300 others in storage. If you stand in the middle of the acres of B-52s, many lying on their bellies with engines or wings missing, and listen to their ailerons creaking and banging in the wind, you feel like you are standing in a giant elephant's graveyard, the place where old bombers go to die. And die they will. The first B-52 went under the guillotine on 1 October 1993.

Amongst the B-52s I found the famous red Boeing NB-52E *56-0632* that was used by the Air Force Flight Dynamics Laboratory for Control Configured Vehicle tests before retirement in 1974. I wondered why it had been removed from 'Celebrity Row' and not shipped to a museum. The answer was not long in coming: the port side of the fuselage appeared to have been blown out by explosives and rendered unsafe to move. A sad waste of a suitable aircraft for preservation.

As a part of the SALT talks, 350 of the B-52s at AMARC are to be cut up on base and thereafter the wrecks will probably be sold for scrap. The wings will be severed from the fuselage which would then be cut in three parts by a 12,000-pound guillotine blade, which is dropped from a 100-foot crane. The Soviets watched a demonstration and decided to use the same method to destroy their own bombers, but with United States officials watching. Destruction is also the fate awaiting most of the 49 Convair F-106 Delta Darts remaining at AMARC. With the demise of the hundreds of F-100 and F-102 remote-controlled drones at various ranges, the F-106 took their place, to be followed eventually by the F-4 Phantom.

The future workload for AMARC will be prodigious; the US Customs has been enquiring about storing fourteen aircraft for an indefinite period; two Boeing 707s are to depart as a part of the JSTARS project; one thousand man-hours will be required to prepare C-130 *55-0026* for overland shipment to Fort Stewart, Florida; and the Army is proposing to store 14,000 armoured personnel carriers and 3,000 trucks at AMARC between now and 1996. The Army is also considering the storage of between 200 and 600 AH-1 Cobra helicopters some time in the near future. Foreign military sales are also in the pipeline, including two C-130Bs for Ecuador, one each for Uruguay and Bolivia, nine F-16s for Pakistan, two F-111Gs for Australia, at least 30 A-4s for Israel, four HH-3 helicopters for Tunisia and 36 A-4s for Argentina. Other possible sales are 50 A-10s to Turkey and ten A-7s to Greece.

And for the remainder of the obsolete aircraft at AMARC? The Air Force is not disposing of unwanted aircraft like it did in the old days. Times are hard for the contractors who own the aircraft scrapyards around the base perimeter. The price of aluminium used to be a dollar a pound; now it has dropped to forty cents. Most of the aircraft resident in the local yards have been there for years, with the exception of Western International. They do a good job restoring aircraft to fly again and a newly-restored and painted ex-Navy C-130 was noted, together with some red and white Navy T-28s in similar condition. Kotz Metals yard contains four derelict P-3s and Bobs Airpark a score of HU-16s, a dozen P-2 Neptunes, various helicopters and four O-2s. Consolidated Aeronautics still have the usual wall to wall S-2 Trackers and E-1 Tracers and DMI Aviation have a field full of C-117s, a few C-97s and two dozen A-4 Skyhawks. Strangely they have been there for at least five years, although they were destined for a foreign government. They have not been demilitarised and one wonders where they will finally end up.

At the end of the day, AMARC is an essential part of the Air Force structure. During Desert Shield and Desert Storm the centre received an influx of orders for spare parts and 1,600 items were shipped out to keep B-52s, F-111s, OV-10s, C-130s, A-7s and P-3s flying. In the fiscal year 1992, AMARC received 996 aircraft and put 762 into storage. It withdrew from storage more than 33,000 parts and 157 aircraft worth $680m. Compared to AMARC's budget of $36.5m this represents a return of more than $18 for each dollar spent. And that is why, fifty years after its inception, the desert boneyard is still there.

As for the rest of the decade? At the rate the US armed forces are contracting we may well soon find more of the Air Force and Navy aircraft strength inside AMARC than outside. It is very likely that AMARC will be busier over the next few years than at any time in its distinguished career, and I look forward to my next visit with keen anticipation.

AMARC INVENTORY – by type and quantity as of March 1994

NAVY (including Marines)

A-3	45
A-4	219
A-6	40
A-7	293
C-1	22
C-2	6
C-118	1
C-130	14
C-131	16
E-2	31
F-4	209
F-8	18
F-14	58
H-1	68
H-2	68
H-3	52
H-34	2
H-53	34
H-57	18
P-2	2
P-3	114
S-2	32
S-3	17
T-1	1
T-2	66
T-28	1
T-33	3
T-34	55
T-39	26
AV-8	41
OV-10	19

TOTAL: 1,591

AIR FORCE

Type	Qty
A-7	240
A-10	183
A-37	15
B-52	298
B-57	26
FB-111	16
YC-14	1
YC-15	1
C-22	2
C-47	1
C-97	1
C-118	6
C-123	25
C-130	86
C-131	16
C-135	90
C-137/Boeing 707	109
C-140	4
C-141	9
GTD-21	14
F-4	891
F-8	9 *
F-15	70
F-16	107
F-84	2
F-100	34
F-101	4
F-102	5
F-105	15
F-106	26
F-111	182
H-1	32
H-3	20
CH-53	19
CH-54	1
O-2	68
P-2	2 *
S-2	1
T-29	4
T-33	104
T-37	89
T-38	157
T-39	27
T-46	2
HU-16	3 *
AV-8	1 *
OV-10	4

TOTAL: 3,021

COAST GUARD

Type	Qty
H-3	36
HH-52	6
HU-25A	3

TOTAL: 45

ARMY

F-10	4 *
UH-1	25
OV-1	31

TOTAL: 60

FINAL TOTAL, ALL SERVICES: 4,717
* Inter-service transfers

Marines Sikorsky CH-53D Sea Stallion *157157* was photographed on the wash rack in August 1993.
(Philip Chinnery)

Lockheed S-3A Viking *160574* arrived
for storage in October 1993 after
service with CVW-2 on the aircraft
carrier USS *Ranger.* *(Philip Chinnery)*

(LEFT)
This Douglas A-4F Skyhawk was flown by the Navy display team 'Blue Angels' and arrived at MASDC in February 1985. Its identity is *154179* and it wears the inventory number 3A532. *(Philip Chinnery)*

(BELOW)
Sikorsky SH-3D Sea King *154118* flew with Navy Helicopter Combat Support Squadron HC-1 and was allocated inventory number 9H023 on arrival in September 1991. *(Philip Chinnery)*

(RIGHT)
Extensive preservation work is required before Navy Sea Cobras take their place in storage. The inventory number 7H233 identifies this AH-1J as *159221* which arrived in March 1993. *(Philip Chinnery)*

(BELOW)
Sikorsky HH-3F *1479* arrived for storage in March 1993 and is one of three dozen Coast Guard H-3s currently at AMARC. *(Philip Chinnery)*

Kaman SH-2F Sea Sprite *151334* last served as 'HT-041' with Navy squadron HSL-30 at Norfolk, Virginia. It arrived in May 1992 and is one of almost 70 of the type now in storage.
(Philip Chinnery)

(ABOVE)
The inventory number TF001 on this Northrop T-38A Talon marks it as the first of its type to arrive for storage. *60-0548* arrived in 1971 and was photographed in the RIT area in late 1993. *(Philip Chinnery)*

(RIGHT)
A newly-arrived Rockwell OV-10 Bronco receives the 'Spraylat' treatment outside the reclamation shed in August 1993. *(Philip Chinnery)*

(LEFT)
One of the stalwarts of the Air Force, the Lockheed T-33 Shooting Star has been represented at AMARC for over thirty years. T-33A *58-0577* arrived in late 1987 and TCD054/*58-0616* in February 1988. *(Philip Chinnery)*

(BELOW)
Rows of Air Force McDonnell F-4 Phantoms, part of the 890 currently in storage. *(Philip Chinnery)*

This Lockheed SP-2H Neptune seen in Bob's Airpark in August 1993 will suffer the same fate as most of the 500 Neptunes which passed through MASDC/AMARC over the last thirty years. *(Philip Chinnery)*

(LEFT)
Almost 190 Douglas A-4 Skyhawks were in storage during the author's recent visit, including two-seater TA-4J trainers *158715* and *158489* which arrived for storage in February 1992. *(Philip Chinnery)*

(Below)
An aerial view of the B-52 fleet at AMARC taken in August 1993, just prior to the start of the elimination process. *(Philip Chinnery)*

Some of the two dozen Convair F-106 Delta Darts still awaiting departure in August 1993 for conversion to remote controlled target drones. A resident since 1984, F-106B *57-2510* is nearest with a former New Jersey Air National Guard machine in the background.
(Philip Chinnery)

The wings and vertical stabilizer have
been removed from this Denver Ports
of Call Boeing 707 since its arrival in
1987. *(Philip Chinnery)*

McDonnell Douglas F-15A Eagle *74-0086* arrived for storage in March 1992 and was allocated inventory number FH016. The orange and black tail markings indicate its previous service with the 199th Tactical Fighter Squadron, Hawaii Air National Guard.
(Philip Chinnery)

(ABOVE)
The badge of the 7th Bombardment Wing adorns this Boeing B-52 Stratofortress, awaiting its fate with others in the RIT area at the end of 1993. *(Philip Chinnery)*

(RIGHT)
Wearing the white and red markings and 'ED' tail code of the Air Force Flight Test Center at Edwards Air Force Base, California, LTV YA-7D Corsair II *67-14582* arrived in late 1992. *(Philip Chinnery)*

Some of the almost 200 Fairchild A-10 Thunderbolt II tank buster aircraft now in storage. This row includes the 'NO' tail markings of the 926th Tactical Fighter Group and the 'DM' of the 355th Tactical Fighter Wing.
(Philip Chinnery)

These Air Force and Navy North American T-39 Sabreliners have suffered extensive spare parts reclamation since their arrival in 1985.

(Philip Chinnery)

(LEFT)
A Soviet Whale? Douglas UA-3B Skywarrior *144834* formerly with Navy Tactical Electronic Warfare Squadron VAQ-34 is one of 45 A-3s in storage. It arrived in September 1990 and was allocated inventory number 2A125. *(Philip Chinnery)*

(BELOW)
Appropriate nose art applied to Boeing B-52G Stratofortress *58-0222*, which served with the 2nd Bombardment Wing, whose motto is 'Libertatem Defendimus', and arrived in the summer of 1992. *(Philip Chinnery)*

(ABOVE)
New residents at AMARC include these Lockheed C-141B Starlifters which arrived in the summer of 1993. The two nearest with yellow stripes on the tail are from the 97th Air Mobility Wing, based at Altus Air Force Base, Oklahoma. *(Philip Chinnery)*

(RIGHT)
With a history stretching back to the Vietnam days of the mid-1960s when they were used as forward air control aircraft, these Cessna O-2A Skymasters may have a promising future elsewhere. Some are heading for Kenya to assist in the war against big game poachers. *(Philip Chinnery)*

The fate which befell *75-0261*, the first Fairchild A-10A Thunderbolt II to be stored at AMARC in December 1990. AC001 is used for Battle Damage Repair Training, along with the other aircraft in the background.

(Philip Chinnery)

A 1993 aerial view across the RIT area
towards the AMARC industrial centre
and headquarters. *(Philip Chinnery)*

The best markings of all the Phantoms at AMARC are worn by RF-4C *66-5843* in 75th Anniversary colours of the 106th Reconnaissance Squadron, Alabama Air National Guard.

(Philip Chinnery)

Cessna T-37B Dragonfly *58-1862* wears
EURO-NATO markings of the Joint Jet
Pilot Training unit, Sheppard AFB,
Texas. Students from NATO countries
send their pilots to the United States
to fly the T-37, T-38 and F-16.
(Philip Chinnery)

(LEFT)
The only Coast Guard Grumman E-2C Hawkeye at AMARC, *160415* arrived in late 1992 and was allocated inventory number 2E023.
(Philip Chinnery)

Grumman C-2A Greyhound *152794*/1C003, which arrived in 1987 from Navy Carrier Transport Squadron VRC-30 is used as a spare parts machine, together with half a dozen E-2 Hawkeyes further down the row. Note the unit badge WE DELIVER FLELOGSUPPRON-30. *(Philip Chinnery)*

(ABOVE)
Surely the most eye-catching aircraft in AMARC. SuperGuppy NASA 940 was converted from a Douglas C-97J Stratofreighter and is listed on the AMARC inventory as *52-2693*/CH626. *(Philip Chinnery)*

(RIGHT)
Almost 60 Grumman F-14A Tomcats have arrived at AMARC since 1990, including *158622*/IK052 that was used for flight test missions with the Pacific Missile Test Center until the end of 1991. *(Philip Chinnery)*

104

An interesting view of some of the
occupants of the Western International
yard outside AMARC, including two
North American T-28 Trojans wearing
Army markings, obviously destined
for civilian warbird operators.
(Philip Chinnery)

(RIGHT)
'Stone Age Mutant Ninja Tanker'
artwork on Boeing KC-135A
Stratotanker *56-3633*, which arrived in
1992. *(Philip Chinnery)*

(BELOW)
Navy Douglas TA-4F Skyhawk
153488, with all previous unit
markings removed, heads a line of
Skyhawks, each seemingly wearing a
different colour scheme. Note the 'bag-
wrapped' Phantom in the distance.
(Philip Chinnery)

Storm clouds gather in the distance for the remains of the Boeing 707 fleet in August 1993. *(Philip Chinnery)*

This row of Phantoms includes many from the Air National Guard. F-4D *64-0968* from the 'Happy Hooligans', the 178th Fighter Interceptor Squadron of the North Dakota Air National Guard, is nearest the camera, next to F-4D *65-0590* from the 171st Fighter Interceptor Squadron, Michigan Air National Guard. *(Philip Chinnery)*

'Bustin Out' nose art on Boeing KC-135A Stratotanker *56-3646*/CA034. Note the badge of the 96th Bomb Wing, an eagle with a bomb in its beak and the motto, 'E Sempre L'Ora' underneath. *(Philip Chinnery)*

(Above)
General Dynamic's F-111A *67-0075* arrived in 1992 and wears the 'SM' tail code of Air Force Materials Commands Sacramento Air Logistics Center at McClellan Air Force Base, California. Other F-111 tail codes noted were 'CC' from the 27th Fighter Wing at Cannon AFB, New Mexico and 'UH' and 'LN' from the 20th and 48th Fighter Wings, withdrawn from the United Kingdom. *(Philip Chinnery)*

(Right)
Cessna OA-37B Dragonfly *69-6438* arrived in 1992 from the 169th Tactical Air Support Squadron, Illinois Air National Guard, after the unit re-equipped with the F-16. The type was used to good effect by the Air Force during the Vietnam war. Pilots used to shut down one of the two engines to allow themselves more loiter time over a target, a feat unique to the type.
(Philip Chinnery)

Visitors to AMARC usually enter along the road at lower right and then turn left along 'Celebrity Row', where unusual and one-off aircraft are displayed whilst in storage. Hundreds of McDonnell F-4 Phantoms are lined up in the background. *(Philip Chinnery)*

Photographed in August 1993, newly arrived General Dynamics F-16A Fighting Falcon *79-0331* begins the preservation process; note the jet exhaust has been sealed. This aircraft has come from the 187th Tactical Fighter Group of the Alabama Air National Guard. Allocated the inventory number FG016, it has since been joined by one hundred more F-16s. *(Philip Chinnery)*